INSPIRATIONS FOR LIFELONG FRIENDSHIPS

Friend to Friend

| TEXT BY | PAINTINGS BY |

DEE APPEL   JACK TERRY

Friend to Friend: Inspirations for Lifelong Friendships
© 2002 by Dee Appel
published by Multnomah Publishers, Inc.
P.O. Box 1720, Sisters, Oregon 97759

ISBN 1-57673-932-5

Artwork © Arts Uniq'®, Inc.
Artwork designs by Jack Terry are reproduced under license from Arts Uniq'®, Inc., Cookeville, Tennessee, and may not be reproduced without permission. For information regarding art prints featured in this book, please contact:

Arts Uniq'®, Inc.   *Jack Terry Fine Art, Ltd.*
P.O. Box 3085   *25251 Freedom Trail*
Cookeville, TN 38502   *Kerrville, TX 78028*
1-800-223-5020   *(830) 367-4242*
                           www.jackterryart.com

Designed by Koechel Peterson & Associates, Minneapolis, Minnesota

Multnomah Publishers, Inc., has made every effort to trace the ownership of all poems and quotes. In the event of a question arising from the use of a poem or quote, we regret any error made and will be pleased to make the necessary correction in future editions of this book.

Scripture quotations are taken from *The Holy Bible,* New International Version © 1973, 1984 by International Bible Society, used by permission of Zondervan Publishing House; *The Holy Bible,* New King James Version (NKJV) © 1984 by Thomas Nelson, Inc.; *The Living Bible* (TLB) © 1971, used by permission of Tyndale House Publishers, Inc., all rights reserved; *Revised Standard Version Bible* (RSV) © 1946, 1952 by the Division of Christian Education of the National Council of the Churches of Christ in the United States of America; *The Holy Bible,* King James Version (KJV).

Multnomah is a trademark of Multnomah Publishers, Inc., and is registered in the U.S. Patent and Trademark Office. The colophon is a trademark of Multnomah Publishers, Inc.

Printed in China

02 03 04 05 06 07 08—10 9 8 7 6 5 4 3 2 1 0

www.multnomahgifts.com

Dedication

The pages that follow only begin to tell how

extraordinarily blessed I've been by the friends God

has placed in my life. I am so grateful to each one

of you for your support, your generosity, your

comfort, and your love. I am who I am today

because of who you have been to me. Thank you

for being the sisters and brothers I never had. You've

given me a taste of God's great love.

You bless my life every single day.

My life has been so blessed by you
I don't know where to start.
The gifts that you have given me
I treasure in my heart.
You've always had a hug to give,
A thoughtful word or deed,
And I could always count on you
Whenever I had need.
I'm grateful to the Lord above
For many things, it's true.
And one that I'm most thankful for
Is that He gave me you.

Table of Contents

One of Life's Richest Blessings

Many kinds of fruits grow upon the tree of life, but none so sweet as friendship.

LUCY LARCOM

Friendship. We all seek it out, and our lives are surely enriched when we are blessed with it. But what exactly is it that draws people together and connects them heart to heart? What makes someone a friend for life? And how do we become the kind of person who can be a good friend to others?

As I pondered these questions, sweet memories of my dear friends washed over me. As I thought about these wonderful people, some of whom I've known for decades and others for only a handful of years, I began to see in them certain attributes that you may have noticed in your own friends: loyalty, trustworthiness, compassion, honesty, kindness, faithfulness, forgiveness, thought-fulness, unconditional love, a heart full of laughter. No wonder friends are among the Lord's greatest gifts and life's sweetest fruits!

Perhaps because I wasn't raised with brothers and sisters, friends have always been especially important to me. The only siblings I have ever known were borne of companion-ship, not lineage. In some ways, I believe that such relationships may be even stronger than family connections because we have chosen each other. Many of my friends and I have grown up together, married and raised families together, and shared life's victories and hard-ships together. We have loved and laughed, played and prayed, wept and celebrated, commiserated and rejoiced—together. We have been partners, companions, roommates, classmates, buddies, pals, chums, and confidants. We have pointed each other to God and held out His truth, believing for one another when the faith of one in our circle faltered, praying for each other when one of us couldn't pray for herself. We have been iron sharpening iron, sisters in Christ, growing closer together and closer to God at the same time. We are friends.

I pray that new friends as well as old are the source of much joy for you—they certainly are for me! May these pages inspire you to enrich those ties that bind you to the ones who often become like family. May you treasure the uniqueness of each of your friends, thanking God for His wonderful creativity and celebrating the gift of who he or she is in your life.

THE ONLY WAY TO HAVE A FRIEND IS TO BE ONE.

RALPH WALDO EMERSON

What comfort to know that someone loves you and will come alongside you in your hour of need. What pleasure to know there is a heart that delights in your successes. What a joy to receive a taste of God's unconditional love this side of heaven. What a blessing to have friends, and indeed what a blessing to be called "friend."

The Gift of Laughter

YOU'RE NEVER TOO OLD FOR SLUMBER PARTIES!

It was a warm evening in late June. The air was filled with the glorious smells of early summer. Enormous pale peach roses from my garden filled the crystal vase on the piano. Freshly picked strawberries nearly overflowed from a ceramic bowl on my kitchen counter. Candles twinkled from various points around the living room, adding their delicate scents to the delightful ambience. The scene was set for a party—a slumber party!

A few years ago it occurred to me that an occasional overnight get-together might be just what some of my friends and I needed: some girlfriend time, a kid-free zone, time to catch up, time to nurture one another—and be nurtured ourselves. No single person would be responsible for a formal meal. Each would bring her favorite dish and share the bounty! Everyone loved the idea, and we set a date.

The doorbell chimed, and my guests began to arrive, toting everything but their own beds. Pillows and sleeping bags. Satchels and duffel bags. Makeup kits and musical instruments. Someone even brought a teddy bear!

We set out all the delectable dishes and decided to get right down to business. Out came the fuzzy slippers and an incredible array of bedtime wear. Just seeing each other's boudoir attire was fun in itself. Soon we were happily settled in front of the fireplace, sharing goodies and painting each other's toenails.

I began telling my friends about a silly poem I was trying to write about golf. I know just enough about golf to be dangerous, which was part of the problem. As I began to repeat the lines from the poem, I got a huge case of the giggles. The more I tried to pull myself together to get to the next line, the worse the giggling got. Then, as often happens with the giggles, even those who hadn't heard what I was saying were caught up in the laughter. We doubled over in hilarious, hearty, can't-catch-your-breath laughter— great gulping guffaws that left us grabbing for tissues to catch the tears that were rolling down our cheeks, sides aching from such exuberant giggling. There is an art to this kind of merriment, and I am blessed to have a goodly number of girlfriends who have perfected it.

By God's design, women have such a yearning for intimacy and relationship. Putting women together in one place dressed in their pajamas is an almost surefire way to get them to let down their hair. In times like these we feel safe and free to "go there." To unlock the child. To get giddy. To speak from the heart. To share long-held secrets that weigh us down. To talk about what God is doing in our life

and to pray, to wait, to trust. Girlfriends understand one another's needs, and we can meet those needs in a variety of healthy ways. But maybe nothing is as healing as laughter.

What an incredible joy to have the kinds of girlfriends who allow me to be a child again! Girlfriends who encourage the playful side of me—and who actually choose to come back again and again. I am so grateful for their love and their acceptance of me just as I am. And sometimes the "who I am" is someone who needs to double over in laughter.

After that first slumber party, I decided to change the invitation to read "pajama party." Should you decide to experiment with this idea, you may certainly call it what you want, but don't count on getting much sleep! What you can count on is the healing balm of laughter, the restorative powers of a cheerful heart just as our Creator has promised. What blessed release!

FORGIVENESS DOES NOT CHANGE THE PAST,
BUT IT DOES ENLARGE THE FUTURE.
PAUL BOESE

My best friend and I have known each other for more than forty-two years. It seems impossible since we both still feel twenty years old. Our friendship has taken us from adolescence to midlife. Through high school, college, and career changes. Through marriage, divorce, and childrearing. Through long separations when we lived half a world apart: she in Panama and I in Oregon—and that was long before e-mail! And, just last year, through the loss of loved ones as we each buried a much-loved parent. During these very full forty-two years, we have at times been apart for months or even years. Still, whenever we get back together, we are always able to pick up just where we left off. Best friends are like that, especially when they're bound together by God's love....

It was my first day of high school at St. Mary's Academy for girls. Scores of young women spilled out of school buses and city buses. Together we formed a sea of crisp, white Peter Pan collars, navy blue sweaters, and stitched-down pleated skirts. Our freshly washed faces were void of even one ounce of makeup lest we be immediately sent to the girl's lavatory to scrub it off. Somehow in that lively crowd, she and I found each other. I immediately saw the Irish in Patty's springy ginger curls—freckles to match—and her cerulean blue eyes. Her infectious laugh was one reason we became fast friends.

We happily discovered that we lived only a short distance apart, so we rode the bus home together from school that day. Thus began our lifelong journey.

Our high school years flew by, each year bringing us the fun of summertime freedom. We were full of the joy of our youth. Since my family lived on a lake, my house was often the meeting place for leisurely days of swimming, waterskiing, boating, badminton competitions, backyard barbecues, or lazy afternoons baking in the hot July sun—long before sunscreen became a summertime staple. The year Patty and I turned sixteen we added boyfriends to the mix. Life was a lot simpler before that happened!

Not long after I had become quite attached to my very first boyfriend, his interest shifted elsewhere.

The target of his growing affections? My best friend. Oh, how that hurt! Young hearts are tender and easily pierced. So for me it was a season of betrayal and loss. Long and tearful telephone calls. Even longer times of absence from each other. It took some time for Patty and me to reconcile, for me to offer forgiveness, for me to offer her the grace Jesus has poured out on me.

One day Patty arrived unexpectedly at my front porch. I could tell by the look on her face that she had something to say. "I'm so sorry, my friend," she told me. "I never, ever meant to hurt you. I've missed you something awful. I need my best friend. Will you forgive me?"

We fell into each other's arms, laughing and weeping in relief.

We realized that boyfriends would come and go, but girlfriends are forever. Our near loss of each other was a very important lesson about life, love, and friendship. Today, of course, Patty and I can clearly see how different we both are from the person that boy grew up to be, and we see the humor in it all. But in the midst of those adolescent relationships, we experienced a very real threat to our friendship.

We have lived a lot of life in the years since then. I've learned that I can count on Patty to tell me the truth in love, to say as painlessly as possible what I need to hear. She knows my flaws and loves me anyway. She encourages me on every step of life's path. We share a deep understanding of who we are in relationship with one another as well as who we are as individuals. If someone were to ask me how our friendship has survived all these years, I would say that, like any other relationship, it has taken staying in touch, fitting in phone conversations, being available to each other in times of need. It has been helped along by prayer and our common love of Jesus. And after all we've shared, Patty is someone who knows me inside out—and still loves me.

Over the years, Patty and I have not been without our disagreements, but the forgiveness we extend to one another has become swift and absolute. Forgiving someone we love is not always easy, but it is essential to lasting relationships. Patty and I learned that important lesson when we were sixteen. We've also seen—maybe you have too—that once forgiveness has been offered and received, you don't look back—except to see how far you've come together.

Be kind to one another,
TENDERHEARTED,
FORGIVING ONE ANOTHER,
even as God in
Christ forgave you.

EPHESIANS 4:32, NKJV

They who forgive most
SHALL BE MOST FORGIVEN.

PHILIP JAMES BAILEY

Sweetened by Time

COUNT YOUR AGE WITH FRIENDS,
BUT NOT WITH YEARS.

Friends come during different seasons of our lives. God plans it that way. Some may remain but a brief time. Others come to stay. They are instantly kindred spirits— fellow travelers on life's journey. Often bound by a common passion, we are entwined in heart, mind, and spirit.

In my own experience, some of the dearest and longest-lasting relationships have been borne of a mutual love of music, that powerful language created by God to communicate what words can't. There is something very special about sharing music with people who understand exactly how you feel. Joy and excitement are intensified as together you explore new lyrics and harmonies. I think that singing with a friend must be like trying an elaborate recipe with a master chef. There is an ahh of satisfaction when you get it right.

I have many fond memories of singing with some very fine musicians. Many I met in college, and though scattered from West Coast to East, we have remained in touch. Several years ago, one of my college friends suggested a reunion of those with whom we had sung and played in years past. Interest was sparked, and we began to look for available dates. Eighteen people, separated by thousands of miles, varying lifestyles, and countless obligations—it was a challenge. But after two years and a myriad of e-mails, we accomplished the seemingly impossible. We would spend an entire week together at the foot of Glacier National Park in Montana.

On a long-awaited afternoon in late August, I pulled into the campground. Handsome log cabins circled its perimeter. The afternoon air was thick with the fragrance of ponderosa pine. It was a beautiful setting, definitely God's country, and I was excited about the chapter of my life that would unfold here.

The others had arrived before me. The in-between years disappeared instantly as my gaze fell upon the smiles of old friends. Contented faces softened by time. Familiar eyes now framed by bifocals. The golden hair of youth fringed with silver. Already comfortably ensconced, a variety of musical instruments at the ready, they all greeted me warmly.

Our conversation took on a staccato-like quality as we fired questions at one another, desperate to learn what had been going on in each other's lives. Together we prepared the evening meal.

As we enjoyed a fabulous barbecue, the sun set fire to the magnificent Rocky Mountains. Soon afterward, many of us enjoyed our first breathtaking night under a wide Montana sky. The crystalline stars set against a blanket of black velvet. The wilderness silence broken only by an occasional coyote call. The purest mountain air. Again, God's spectacular handiwork was a perfect setting for a reunion concert.

Out came the guitars, banjos, mandolin, fiddle, and bass. As if we'd never been apart, a chord was struck. Eighteen voices blended in splendid bluegrass harmonies. What an explosion of joy in my heart! We reached back nearly thirty years and began a journey of remembrance as each of us grabbed a phrase from a favorite song. Everyone else quickly joined in. Our week was filled with wonderful warm memories and many delightful hours of music. Those seven days were a celebration and renewal of longtime friendships.

Somehow, just seeing old friends gives a kind of continuity to life. It is reassuring to discover that some things don't change. And it is comforting to learn that the things that do change often change for all of us. Each of us forgot words, lost chords, and failed in our attempts to recall the specifics of certain events. But we were able to laugh at our forgetfulness, our waning youth, and our not-so-quick reflexes.

The time passed all too quickly, and suddenly the week was over. As we began our sad farewells, we agreed that despite the miles that separate us, we are all on this road of life together. Though we've gone in a variety of directions, we are still connected in many ways. The memories of our youth are now intertwined with those of the more recent past. Rekindled is the love we have for each other as friends. And that is the sweetest kind of melody to have lingering in our hearts, binding us together in lifelong friendships.

Think about people with whom you have shared a chapter or two of your life. If you have an opportunity to reunite with them, don't let it pass you by. Oh, you may count on being with them in heaven, but don't wait. There is much comfort to be found in the company of old friends, and the joy of reunion will be well worth the effort.

The years teach much
WHICH THE DAYS NEVER KNEW.

RALPH WALDO EMERSON

A friend is dearer than the light of heaven;
for it would be better for us that the sun were extinguished,
than that we should be without friends.

SAINT CHRYSOSTOM

The best antique
IS AN OLD FRIEND.

AUTHOR UNKNOWN

A friend may well BE RECKONED THE *masterpiece of nature.*

RALPH WALDO EMERSON

Friendship is a union of spirits,
a marriage of hearts,
and the bond thereof virtue.

WILLIAM PENN

EVERY ACTION IS MEASURED BY THE DEPTH
OF THE SENTIMENT FROM WHICH IT PROCEEDS.

RALPH WALDO EMERSON

As I walk through my home and see gifts from cherished friends, I am reminded of the blessings bestowed in my life. In a moment of darkness or loneliness, such a reminder can bring great encouragement and hope, a timely reminder of God's presence with us always.

My friend Patty's mother, Marjorie, has always been a great friend and a second mom to me. She is a wonderful watercolorist. Her paintings are vibrant and full of life, just like her. No one knows for sure how old she is. We're not allowed to discuss it, and we don't think her doctor even knows. Marjorie stays young by living. To keep herself physically fit, she plays golf. To keep mentally fit, she plays bridge. To keep her spirits high, she paints.

When my own mother's health began to fail, Marjorie wanted to cheer her up. Among the things on Mother's list of "favorites" were pink dogwood trees. In fact, they were very close to the top. So years ago, when my family moved from the lake, it was no surprise that one of the first things Mother did at the  new house was plant a pink dogwood tree. For her, its soft-petaled blossoms were silent messengers from God, quietly signaling the sure coming of spring and always bringing her hope. Marjorie knew that, so she painted Mother a dogwood that would give her springtime hope throughout the year.

My mother loved that painting. It hung in a place of honor in her assisted-living apartment. She could always see it from her recliner. It was one of the few things that went with her when she became so ill that we had to move her to the infirmary. And it was leaning against the window by her bed when she quietly slipped away in her sleep into her heavenly Father's arms.

Sometimes when I miss my mother the most, I sit in my bedroom and admire Marjorie's painting. It now hangs in a special corner near my bed. That thoughtful and generous gift sweetly reminds me of Mother and her gentle heart, the soft touch of her hand, her constant reassurance. And these thoughts encourage me because I know that Mother, who always found a way to look toward spring, now enjoys an eternal spring with her Creator.

As if these thoughts of Mother weren't gift enough, pointing me as they do to God, I am doubly blessed when I see the artist's signature in the corner. There are some squiggly lines next to Marjorie's name. Not everyone would recognize them. But I took shorthand. They read, "I love you." Such a blessing—first to my mother's failing heart and today to my lonely one.

WHEN SHE HAD PASSED,
IT SEEMED LIKE
THE CEASING OF
EXQUISITE MUSIC.

HENRY WADSWORTH LONGFELLOW

HOW CAN I FIND THE SHINING WORD... THAT TELLS ALL THAT YOUR LOVE HAS MEANT TO ME.

GRACE NOLL CROWELL

We are all busy these days. Living without a daily planner seems impossible. Days and weeks roar past us, full speed ahead. It seems that the only way I can keep up with my beloved friends is to make a date with them. I have found that inviting them for tea is the perfect way to bring life to a pleasurable standstill.

My auntie started my teacup collection when I was eight. She traveled a great deal, and I remember my excitement over the periodic arrival of plain brown parcels decorated with colorful stamps. The packages were often embellished with fascinating characters and symbols from faraway countries. Truthfully, at eight I was more enchanted with the packaging than the contents. All these years later, though, I am thrilled whenever I take one of those fine china cups from my curio cabinet. I carefully turn them over in my hands: Royal Albert, Paragon, Limoges. One even reads, "Handpainted, occupied Japan." Each is rich with its own history and its own gift of relaxation.

The exquisite teacups offer a perfect opportunity to bless my friends, to share the good gifts that God has given me. So, when I have company over for tea, I choose an assortment of my treasured cups. Then I ask my guests to select their favorite. Some friends are hesitant to handle the fragile china. I assure each that she is far more precious to me than any cup and saucer. What a great loss it would be to keep the treasures safe but untouched in my antique cabinet! By the way, if we're not careful, we can do that with treasured friendships as well.

Some of my sweetest moments with a friend have been over a well-brewed cup of tea. There is a calmness in the ceremony of tea. A natural serenity that accompanies the ritual: dainty spoons, sandwiches of cucumber and cream cheese, sweets and savories, fresh-cut flowers complementing a lacy tablecloth. With a shared sigh of contentment, we reconnect with one another.

Over the years dear friends have added some beautiful pieces to my original collection. Whenever I bring out one of these "pretties" to have tea with a girlfriend, I feel unbelievably blessed. Each cup, like each friend, is a testimony of God's generous goodness to me. So, as I prepare the tea, anticipating the time we will spend together, I take great delight in sharing my teacup blessings. I like to think of them as holding a cupful of love, a cupful of God's love that is given to us in order to be shared with others. Then, as I pour some tea into those china treasures, I savor the friendship that refreshes.

Pleasant words
ARE LIKE A HONEYCOMB,
sweetness to the soul
AND HEALTH TO THE BODY.

PROVERBS 16:24, RSV

Give generously,
FOR YOUR GIFTS
will return to you later.

ECCLESIASTES 11:1, TLB

Our friends see
THE BEST IN US,
and by that very fact,
CALL FORTH THE BEST FROM US.

BLACK

'Tis something to be
WILLING TO COMMEND;
But my best praise is,
THAT I AM YOUR FRIEND.

SOUTHERNE

In friendship there
is nothing false,
and nothing pretended;
and whatever belongs to it
is sincere and spontaneous.

CICERO

A Heart of Compassion

IN FRIENDSHIP YOUR HEART IS LIKE A BELL STRUCK EVERY TIME YOUR FRIEND IS IN TROUBLE.

HENRY WARD BEECHER

Five years ago I went through a very dark valley. I had discovered a lump in my breast. My life was turned upside down in the time it took the surgeon to say one word—carcinoma. Shock and panic rocked me to my core. I flew through emotions like a feather in a whirlwind. Denial. Anger. Pain. Despondency. Fear. And, at times, the desperate question "God, where are You? Why is this happening?"

My children were already grown and, for the most part, out on their own. So I faced an unknown future and a *lot* of decisions to make in a very short time. They were extremely scary decisions, too. They came with words like *mastectomy* and *radical, chemotherapy* and *radiation*. I networked with others who had walked this same path. I read everything I could in two short weeks. Mostly I prayed day and night. I knew none of this surprised God and I knew it wasn't too much for Him to handle, but I still had to walk through it. At last, I made a choice: surgery, followed by eight months of chemotherapy.

Six weeks passed after a successful lumpectomy. My first chemo treatment was arranged. I was beyond terrified. My body is very sensitive to medications, and I am prone to allergic reactions. My imagination went into overdrive. What would it be like? How would it feel? Would my heart stop the moment the needle began to release its powerful chemicals?

I wrote good-bye letters to each of my children. I updated my will. I put my house and personal papers in order. I geared up mentally to face the monster head on. *Alone.*

But then, about a week before my first treatment, the phone rang. It was Linda, one of my closest friends from church. "Dee, may I go with you to your appointment?" she asked. I was struck by the way she asked the question. It wasn't "Do you want me to go?" or "Do you need me to go?" She made me feel as if it would be her *privilege* to go with me. I was overwhelmed.

Linda attended that first session with me. She held my right hand as the nurse fed the IV line into my left arm. She read to me and distracted me with lighthearted stories. She prayed with me. She prayed for me. She let me cry. She cried with me. And she didn't leave my side for five long and terrifying hours. Through that first awful session—and every single one that followed for the next eight months— there was my steadfast friend. Her presence was compassion incarnate, an act of intense loyalty. To me, she was God with flesh and bones. Her firm faith in the Lord, in His power and His goodness, and her commitment to me gave me courage to face each new treatment. Her love got me through.

We can do so much to lighten one another's burdens. A phone call. A postcard. A prayer. A flower from the garden. A meal delivered to the doorstep. And last but not least, simple companionship. Linda gave me the gifts of her energy, her time, herself. In the process, she taught me a huge lesson about love and compassion. When we are hurting, there is nothing as comforting as the hand of a friend. I am so grateful for her hand that held mine. Thank you, my dear friend, from the bottom of my heart.

A real friend is one
WHO WALKS IN WHEN
the rest of the world walks out.
WALTER WINCHELL

Let love be your

greatest aim.

Giving is so often thought of
in terms of the things we give,
but our greatest giving is of
our time, and kindness,
and even comfort for
those who need it.
We look on these gifts
as unimportant—
until we need them.

JOYCE SEQUICHIE HIFLER

The Faces of Kindness

LIFE IS SHORT, AND WE HAVE NEVER TOO MUCH TIME
FOR GLADDENING THE HEARTS OF THOSE WHO ARE
TRAVELING THE DARK JOURNEY WITH US.

HENRI FREDERIC AMIEL

Generosity, goodness, grace, compassion, warmth, understanding, benevolence, comfort. Kindness wears many faces, doesn't it? When we are ill, it may arrive in the form of a warm meal delivered by a caring neighbor. Or perhaps it comes as a friend's offer to watch our little ones so we can have a special evening out. Sometimes, when life has dealt a particularly hard blow, kindness appears in unique and unexpected ways.

In December 1998, our family home was ravaged by fire. It was one of the coldest winters in Oregon's recent history, and I faced the overwhelming task of inventorying our personal belongings. When I arrived that morning, icicles hung in the spaces where windows used to be. The house was freezing cold. What was left of our Christmas tree leaned precariously from its stand. Soggy and singed gifts toppled one over the other, sitting sadly among a mix of wet couch pillows, tangled tree lights, and smoke-stained art.

As I slogged through the rubble, my heart was heavy. I was practically immobilized, overwhelmed by all the memories that lingered in this place. I had raised my children here; we had lived a lot of life within these walls. Now I stood in the middle of the room that was once my kitchen and began to dig through the charred remains of twenty-two years.

I had opened just a few of the cupboards when I heard a car pull into the driveway. I made my way to the door. There stood Patty, my longtime friend and my personal angel of mercy. As we hugged each other, I saw another vehicle pull in. And another. Word had spread. There were ten cars in all—ten dear friends prepared to do battle with sludge and grime. Patty, ever the administrator and wise in the ways of inventory, presented clipboards, pens, colored tags, and plastic bags to this generous and good-hearted army. "Upstairs bathroom," she called as she handed out supplies. "Hallway closet." "Back bedroom." One by one she assigned the areas. What blessed relief flooded my soul!

Kindness has come to my door on many occasions in my lifetime, but that day is one that will forever be engraved on my heart. These women served with humility and joy just as Jesus did. The sacrificial love of those dear women carried me through. That is the stuff lifelong relationships are made of. I strive to be that kind of friend.

Kindness wears the sweetest face when it wears the face of friendship.

Give what you have to someone—
IT MAY BE BETTER
than you dare to think.

HENRY WADSWORTH LONGFELLOW

In friendship there
IS NOTHING FALSE,
and nothing pretended;
AND WHATEVER
belongs to it is
SINCERE AND SPONTANEOUS

CICERO

There is in friendship
something of all relations,
and something above them all.
It is the golden thread that
ties the hearts of all the world.

EVELYN

HEARTS ARE LINKED TO HEARTS BY GOD.

THE FRIEND ON WHOSE FIDELITY YOU CAN COUNT,

WHOSE SUCCESS IN LIFE FLUSHES YOUR CHEEK WITH HONEST SATISFACTION,

WHOSE TRIUMPHANT CAREER YOU HAVE TRACED AND READ

WITH A HEART THROBBING ALMOST AS IF IT WERE A THING ALIVE,

FOR WHOSE HONOUR YOU WOULD ANSWER AS FOR YOUR OWN;

THAT FRIEND, GIVEN TO YOU BY CIRCUMSTANCES OVER WHICH

YOU HAVE NO CONTROL, WAS GOD'S OWN GIFT.

F. W. ROBERTSON